The Classic Guitar Collection. Volume Three

Edited by Leonid Bolotine.
This album was formerly distributed under the title
'Classical Guitar', Everybody's Favourite Series Number 119.

D0523136

DATE DUE

AG/4/03			

DEMCO 38-296

Riverside Community College
Library
4800 Magnolia Avenue
Riverside, CA 92506

AMSCO
NEW YORK • LONDON • SYDNEY

M 125 .C46 1977 v.3

The Classic guitar
collection

Published 1977 by
Amsco Music Publishing Company
(a division of Music Sales Limited,
8/9 Frith Street, London W1V 5TZ.)
London, New York, Sydney

Cover illustration by Adrian George
Designed by Pearce Marchbank

All arrangements copyright © 1977 Dorsey Brothers Limited
(a division of Music Sales Limited, 8/9 Frith Street, London W1V 5TZ.)

This album copyright © 1977 by Amsco Publishing Company
(a division of Music Sales Limited, 8/9 Frith Street, London W1V 5TZ.)

Order No. AM 32673
US International Standard Book Number: 0.8256.2270.0
UK International Standard Book Number: 0.86001.453.3

Exclusive Distributors:
Music Sales Corporation
257 Park Avenue South, New York, NY 10010, USA
Music Sales Limited
8/9 Frith Street, London W1V 5TZ, England
Music Sales Pty. Limited
120 Rothschild Street, Rosebery, Sydney, NSW 2018, Australia

Printed in the United States of America by
Vicks Lithograph and Printing Corporation

Nine Country Dances.

Anon.

2.

© Copyright 1963 Amsco Music Publishing Company   All Rights Reserved

3.

4.

5.

6.

7.

8.

9.

Two Minuets.

Anon.

© Copyright 1963 Amsco Music Publishing Company   All Rights Reserved

Five Easy Pieces.

Ferdinando Carulli
(1770-1841)

2.

© Copyright 1963 Amsco Music Publishing Company   All Rights Reserved

3.

Andante grazioso

Fine

D.C. al Fine

10

4.

Poco allegretto quasi andante

D.C. al Fine

5.

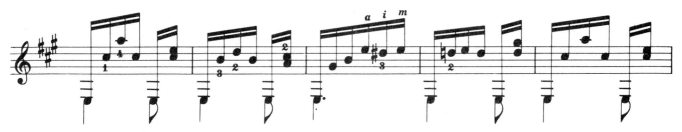

Fine

D.C.
al.Fine

Three Easy Sonatinas.

Ferdinando Carulli

© Copyright 1963 Amsco Music Publishing Company   All Rights Reserved

2.

Introduction

Moderato

Andante

14

3.

Introduction

Moderato

Andante

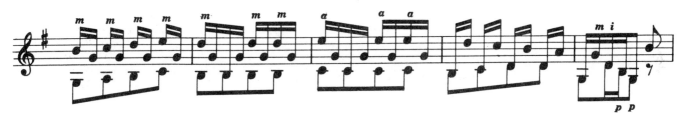

Ten Easy Pieces.

Antonio Diabelli, Op. 89
(1781-1858)

Andante

© Copyright 1963 Amsco Music Publishing Company   All Rights Reserved

Minuet

2.

Moderato cantabile

Trio

Fine

D.C. al Fine.

3.

19

Allemande
4.

5.

Moderato con giusto

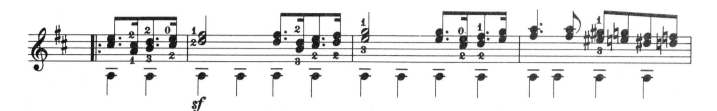

6.

Andante cantabile

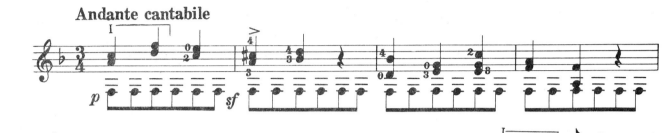

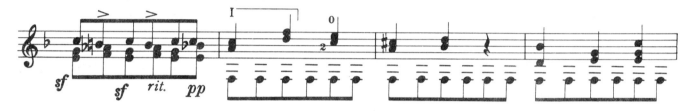

Scherzo
7.

Trio

Scherzo da capo al Fine.

Rondo
8.

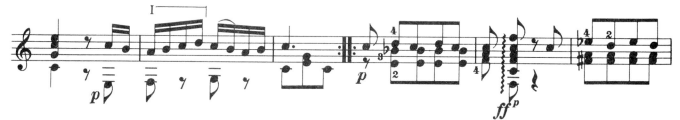

9.

Allegretto

Marcia
10.

Maestoso

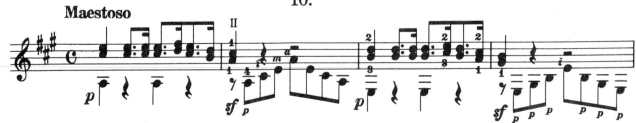

Country Dances.

Antonio Diabelli
Op.127

2.

© Copyright 1963 Amsco Music Publishing Company   All Rights Reserved

3.

4.

5.

6.

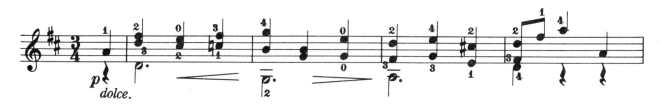

7.

8.

9.

10.

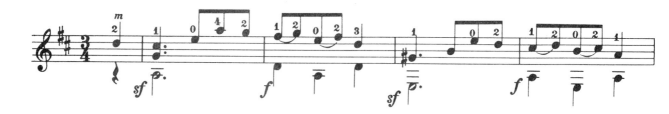

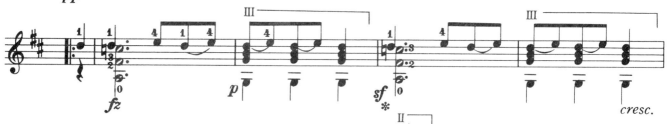

11.

12.

Bourrée.

Johann Krieger
(1651-1735)

Minuet.

Johann Krieger

© Copyright 1963 Amsco Music Publishing Company   All Rights Reserved

Incomparable.

Anon.

Bourrée.

Leopold Mozart
(1719-1787)

© Copyright 1963 Amsco Music Publishing Company   All Rights Reserved

Pavana.

Grave - maestoso

Luis Milan
(1500 - 1561)

Minuet.

Johann Sebastian Bach
(1685 - 1750)

© Copyright 1963 Amsco Music Publishing Company   All Rights Reserved

Aria.

Johann Sebastian Bach
*(from the Notebook of Anna Magdalena Bach)

Andante con moto

Minuetto.

J. Chr. Friedrich Bach
(1732-1795)

Ⓒ Copyright 1963 Amsco Music Publishing Company   All Rights Reserved

Minuet.

Johann Sebastian Bach
(from the Notebook of Anna Magdalena Bach)

Lute Prelude.

Johann Sebastian Bach
(1685 - 1750)

© Copyright 1963 Amsco Music Publishing Company   All Rights Reserved

Song.

Anon.

Andante

Allemande.

Joseph Haydn
(1732-1809)

© Copyright 1963 Amsco Music Publishing Company   All Rights Reserved

Petite Pièce.

Allegro

Wolfgang Amadeus Mozart
(1756-1791)

© Copyright 1963 Amsco Music Publishing Company   All Rights Reserved

Thirty-Two Pieces.

Mauro Giuliani
(1781-1828)

Andantino

2.

Grazioso

© Copyright 1963 Amsco Music Publishing Company   All Rights Reserved

3.

Allegretto

4.

Grazioso

5.

Allegretto

6.

Allegro

7.

8.

9.

Andantino

10.

Allegro

11.

Grazioso

12.

Allegretto

13.

Allegro

14.

Andantino

15.

Allegretto

16.

Vivace

17.

Larghetto

18.

Allegretto

19.

Tempo di Polacca

20.

Allegretto

21.

Andantino

piu mosso

22.

Allegretto

23.

Grazioso

24.

Allegro

25.

Andantino Grazioso

26.

27.

28.

29.

Allegretto

30.

Andantino

31.

Allegretto

32.

59

Six Caprices.

Moderato

Matteo Carcassi, Op. 26
(1792 - 1853)

© Copyright 1963 Amsco Music Publishing Company   All Rights Reserved

2.

Vivace

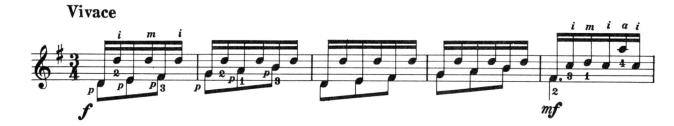

3.

Moderato con espression

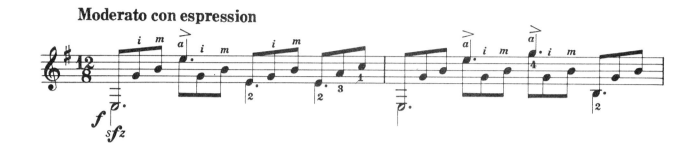

4.

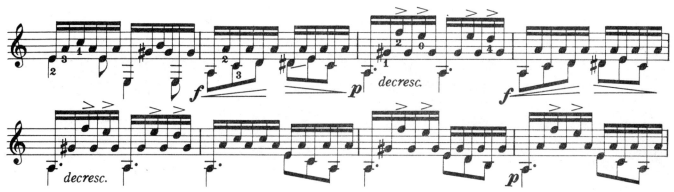

5.

Allegro

6.

Allegro non troppo

71

Etude.

Matteo Carcassi

Allegretto

© Copyright 1963 Amsco Music Publishing Company   All Rights Reserved

Etude.

Andantino

Matteo Carcassi

© Copyright 1963 Amsco Music Publishing Company   All Rights Reserved

Sonatine.

Filippo Gragnani, Op. 6
(1740-1800)

Andante sostenuto

© Copyright 1963 Amsco Music Publishing Company   All Rights Reserved

Etude on a Theme
by Mozart.

Ferdinando Carulli

© Copyright 1963 Amsco Music Publishing Company   All Rights Reserved

Theme and Variation.

Beethoven · Carulli

© Copyright 1963 Amsco Music Publishing Company   All Rights Reserved

Grand Etude.

Ferdinando Carulli

© Copyright 1963 Amsco Music Publishing Company   All Rights Reserved

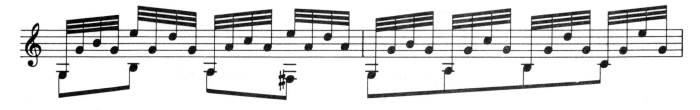

Etude.

Fernando Sor
(1778-1839)

Andante

© Copyright 1963 Amsco Music Publishing Company   All Rights Reserved

Sonata.

Ferdinando Carulli

© Copyright 1963 Amsco Music Publishing Company   All Rights Reserved

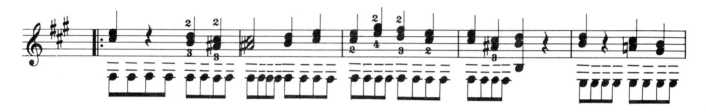

Rondo Allegro

Tempest.

Ferdinando Carulli

Allegro

© Copyright 1963 Amsco Music Publishing Company   All Rights Reserved

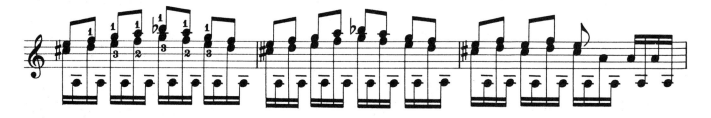

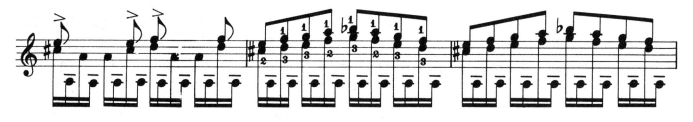

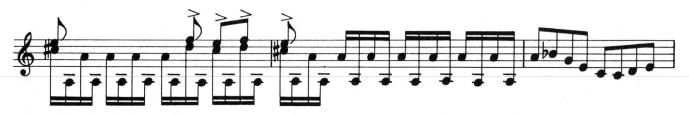

D. C.